Contents

INTRODUCTION

Understanding of ADHD in Children And Adults: The brain communicates messages through neurons in the brain. But at the end of every neuron there is a gap called a synapse. The message needs to jump between the gaps, and does this with the aid of a chemical called a neurotransmitter produced by the body. "Persons with ADHD tend not to release enough of these essential chemicals, or to release and reload them too quickly before an adequate connection has been made." In effect, messages struggle to get where they need to go to be acted on. Medications, including stimulants and non-stimulants, help make up for these deficits by triggering the release of certain chemicals, which in turn help the neurons to communicate with each other.

Currently, the Diagnostic and Statistical Manual (DSM-IV) of Mental Health Disorders—the handbook used by mental health professionals to assess and diagnose ADHD—does not include supporting information on the link between ADHD and emotion regulation.

Finally, it's important to highlight that while a person with ADHD will struggle with a variety of symptoms that fall under inattention and/or impulsivity and hyperactivity, in almost every case there will be areas where the person is able to focus intently, sometimes referred to as "hyper-focus." This is typically seen in areas that the person shows a great interest in, such as playing video games, playing a musical instrument or even reading when the subject matter has great appeal.

If you or someone you love suffers from ADHD (Attention Deficit/Hyperactivity Disorder), you've probably spent what feels like a lifetime searching for a treatment that reduces the symptoms without all the negative side effects. Now, you can stop looking. CBD oil might be just the solution you've been hoping for. If you're curious about using CBD oil for ADHD, you've come to the right place.

Attention-Deficit Hyperactivity Disorder (ADHD) is a neurodevelopmental condition that affects both children and adults.

Almost eleven percent of American children have ADHD. But it's not just a childhood disorder. About four percent of American adults have ADHD as well. It is thought to be genetic, with some environmental factors playing a role as well. ADHD is more prevalent in children living in lower-income households, which suggests that environment is indeed significant.

There is a long tradition of people with ADHD using CBD and other cannabis products to treat their condition. While it may seem counterintuitive to some, this is mainly because of the psychoactive properties associated with the THC in cannabis. The non-psychoactive CBD, however, has shown results in managing ADHD.

While there is not a ton of research into CBD oil as a treatment for ADHD, the studies done thus far have been promising. Since CBD also has the effects of improving mood and decreasing anxiety, which are often present in sufferers of ADHD, it is likely to have positive results even if it does not affect the underlying disorder.

More research is necessary to determine whether CBD will become a mainstream treatment for ADHD. Controlled studies should be conducted in the near future, due to the medical field's current interest in CBD, as well as increasing legality making such studies possible.

ADHD

Attention-Deficit Hyperactivity Disorder (ADHD) is a neurodevelopmental condition that affects both children and adults. ADHD develops when the brain and central nervous system suffer impairments related to growth and development. A person with ADHD will show varying degrees of these three behaviors: inattention, impulsivity and hyperactivity.

Causes of ADHD

It's not clear what exactly causes ADHD, though there are factors that may increase the chances of developing the condition. While researchers haven't identified a specific ADHD gene, lots of studies show a genetic link. It's quite common for a person diagnosed with ADHD to have at least one close relative with the condition Environmental factors may also play a role. These include exposure to pesticides and lead, a brain injury, being born prematurely or with a low birth weight.

Diagnosis of ADHD

ADHD is often diagnosed in childhood, and typically continues through adolescence and into adulthood. The level of impairment can vary from person to person and from one situation to another; symptoms can lessen or increase over time.

According to a 2015 National Health Statistics Report issued by the U.S. Department of Health and Human Services, parents reported a total of 6.4 million school age children between ages 4 and 17 having ever been diagnosed with ADHD. This works out to be 11 percent of children, or roughly one in 10 kids.

The rate of boys diagnosed with ADHD is three times higher than the number of girls diagnosed. And according to the National Institute of Mental Health, the average age for diagnosis when parents reported a child with moderate symptoms of ADHD was 7 years old. In instances where parents reported their child had more severe ADHD symptoms, the age for diagnosis was 5. Mild symptoms are diagnosed more often at age 8.

Meanwhile, 4 percent of the adult population, or 8 million adults, are estimated to have ADHD. When you compare this to the number of children and adolescents, the total number of adults reporting ADHD drops by more than half. This may be due to the fact that as a total population, fewer adults overall have been screened for the condition. Additionally, symptoms of ADHD can lessen in adulthood due to maturation of the brain. Adults with ADHD may also find themselves in jobs where their particular challenges are supported or don't factor in to overall performance. The same thing can be said of a supportive spouse who might take over paying bills from the partner with ADHD, and making sure important appointments are scheduled and kept. Overall, of those who are diagnosed as children and teenagers, an estimated 15% of adults still meet the criteria for ADHD, according to the National Center for Health Statistics.

Getting Diagnosed

In order to meet the diagnostic criteria for ADHD for children, there need to be six or more symptoms that have frequently and significantly impacted their lives in two or more settings (school, social, or home) for at least six months. These symptoms must be more excessive than what would be appropriate for the child's age and developmental level. For anyone who is 17 years old or older, there must be five or more symptoms that have had a frequent and detrimental effect on two or more settings (school, social, home, or work). Symptoms also must have started before you were 12 years old.

If you think you or your child may have ADHD, talk to your doctor. He or she can either diagnose you or recommend a mental health professional who can. Getting treatment like medication, therapy, or a combination of both can help pave the way to more success at work, school, home, and in relationships.

ADHD Symptoms in Adults and Children

Attention-deficit hyperactivity disorder (ADHD) is a condition that people discuss a lot these days, often ascribing the term casually to persons who seem unusually frenetic, "flaky," or scattered.

But, as a medical condition, it is not so easily ascribed. Parents will often struggle to distinguish between what might be considered "normal" rambunctiousness and inattention and the genuine inability to sit still and focus. Even untrained physicians

8

can have difficulty with this given that there is no single test that can diagnose ADHD or similar behavioral or learning disorders.

Ultimately, to make the distinction, pediatricians will run through a checklist of characteristic symptoms to determine whether the child meets the criteria for ADHD as outlined in the American Psychiatric Association's Diagnostic and Statistical Manual of Mental Disorders, Fifth Edition (DSM-5).

Presentations of ADHD

There are three presentations, or subtypes, of ADHD, including:

ADHD, predominantly inattentive presentation: Symptoms are primarily related to inattention. The individual does not display significant hyperactive/impulsive behaviors. This type tends to be more common in females.

ADHD, predominantly hyperactive-impulsive presentation: Symptoms are primarily related to hyperactivity and impulsivity. The individual does not display significant attention problems. This type tends to be more common in males.

ADHD, combined presentation: The individual displays both inattentive and hyperactive/impulsive symptoms.

Symptoms of ADHD

The core symptoms of attention-deficit/hyperactivity disorder (ADHD) include inattention, hyperactivity, and impulsivity. Difficulties with concentration, mental focus, and inhibition of impulses and behaviors are chronic and pervasive and impair an individual's daily functioning across various settings home, school, or work as well as in relationships with others. Though it's more common in children, affecting an estimated 8.4 percent, ADHD affects as many as 2.5 percent of adults as well.

A child or adult with ADHD will show varying degrees of these three behaviors: inattention, impulsivity and hyperactivity.

However, it's important to mention that any child or adult— meaning even people without ADHD—will demonstrate one or more of these associated behaviors at any given time. Most people with ADHD will experience a combination of symptoms from each of the subtypes—inattention and hyperactivity/impulsivity. When signs of inattention, impulsivity and hyperactivity are seen for at least 6 months and demonstrated in more than one setting, such as the home, classroom or at work, ADHD may be the cause.

A diagnosis of ADHD in a child age 16 or younger should be considered when he or she presents with six or more symptoms of inattention and/or hyperactivity and impulsivity that are characterized as inappropriate for their developmental level. Examples of these symptoms are outlined, below.

From age 17 and up, a clinician will look for 5 or more symptoms of inattention and/or impulsivity and hyperactivity that are developmentally inappropriate.

Symptoms of Inattention:

- frequent difficulty focusing on tasks, including homework or meeting work deadlines
- often struggles to follow through on projects, assignments, and chores
- has difficulty staying organized and misses deadlines
- is often easily distracted
- often fails to respond when being spoken to
- has difficulty keeping track of important items such as keys, cell phone, homework assignment pad.

Symptoms of impulsivity and hyperactivity:

- lacks careful thought/does not consider the potential consequences before acting on something or expressing one's feelings
- abnormally active and/or disruptive behavior
- talks excessively
- struggles to be quiet during leisure activities
- finds it difficult to wait his turn
- squirms in his seat; fidgets with his hands and feet.

Another way a doctor may evaluate and categorize symptoms is by grouping them into categories. Dr. Brown's research has pinpointed how the symptoms of cognitive function impairment caused by ADHD tend to show up in six clusters. These include: activation, focus, effort, emotion, memory and action.

For instance, initiating and organizing tasks, fall under "activation" and difficulty completing tasks or sustaining effort fall under "effort." Under effort is also regulating alertness—a person with ADHD may not be able to quiet their mind enough to fall asleep when they should.

Less often described in ADHD literature is the "emotion cluster." Dr. Brown, who's assessed and treated patients with ADHD for more than 25 years, says they often report difficulty with managing emotions that include anger, worry, frustration, and disappointment. These create additional challenges for the person with ADHD.

Symptoms May Vary

Previously known as ADD, symptoms of ADHD are typically seen early in a child's life, often when he or she enters a school setting. Though plenty of kids outgrow it, ADHD may continue into adolescence and adulthood, particularly the inattentive type. Many adults don't realize they have ADHD because they weren't diagnosed as children. By the time you reach adulthood, you have likely learned ways to cope better with your symptoms and you may even have outgrown some of them, especially hyperactive ones. Because of these factors, your symptoms won't necessarily be as obvious a child's, but if you think back to your childhood, you'll probably recognize yourself since all adults with ADHD had it as children.

Here's a more detailed look at the three hallmark symptoms of ADHD.

➢ Inattention

Children and adults who are inattentive have difficulty staying focused and attending to tasks that they perceive as mundane. Because of this, they may procrastinate doing their homework or work since there is a great deal of mental energy needed to complete it. They are easily distracted by irrelevant sights and sounds, shift from one activity to another, and seem to get bored easily. They may appear forgetful and even spacey or confused as if they're in a fog or living in a different world in their own heads. They may not seem like they're listening when they're being spoken to. Organizing and completing tasks is often extremely difficult, as is sorting out what information is relevant versus what's irrelevant.

If you have inattentive symptoms, you may have great difficulty keeping up with school work or bills, frequently lose things, and live your life in a disorganized way. Following through on promises and commitments may be a struggle and time management is also often an issue. Inattentive behaviors are often overlooked because they're harder to identify and less disruptive than hyperactive and impulsive symptoms, so kids with these symptoms may slip through the cracks. An individual with the predominantly inattentive presentation of ADHD may even appear sluggish, lethargic, and slow to respond and process information.

➢ Hyperactivity

Hyperactivity is the symptom most people think of when they hear the term "ADHD." Children and adults who are hyperactive have excessively high levels of activity, which may present as physical and/or verbal overactivity. They may appear to be in constant motion and perpetually on the go as if driven by a motor. They have difficulty keeping their bodies still—moving about excessively, squirming, or fidgeting.

People who are hyperactive often feel restless, especially if they're adults or teens. They may talk excessively, interrupt others, and monopolize conversations, not letting others talk. It's not unusual for an individual with hyperactive symptoms to engage in a running commentary on the activities going on around them. Their behaviors tend to be loud and disruptive. This difficulty regulating their own activity level often creates great problems in social, school, and work situations.

> Impulsivity

Children and adults who are impulsive have trouble inhibiting their behaviors and responses. They often act and speak before thinking, reacting in a rapid way without considering consequences. They may interrupt others, blurt out responses, and rush through assignments or forms without carefully reading or listening to instructions. Waiting for their turn and being patient is extremely difficult for people who are impulsive. They prefer speed over accuracy and so they often complete tasks quickly but in a careless manner. They go full swing into situations and may even place themselves in potentially risky situations without thought. Their lack of impulse control can not only be dangerous but it can also create stress at school or work and in relationships with others. Delayed gratification or waiting for larger rewards is very hard for an impulsive person.

➢ Comorbid Conditions

As many as one-third of children with ADHD have one or more coexisting, or comorbid, conditions. The most common of these are behavioral problems, anxiety, depression, and learning and language disabilities. Adults with ADHD show an even higher incidence of comorbid disorders. These adults may also suffer from depression, bipolar disorder, substance abuse disorders, anxiety disorders, or behavioral problems.

Distinguishing the Types of ADHD

ADHD symptoms are typically grouped into two major categories: inattention (the inability to stay focused) and hyperactivity-impulsivity (impulsive behaviors that are excessive and disruptive). The determination of ADHD is largely based on whether the behaviors are appropriate or inappropriate for the child's developmental age.

The range of symptoms can vary from child to child and lead to a variety of different diagnoses broadly classified as follows:

- Predominantly inattentive type ADHD describes a child who has trouble paying attention but isn't hyperactive or impulsive.
- Predominantly hyperactive-impulsive type ADHD defined as excessive restlessness, rashness, and fidgetiness without the characteristic lack of focus.

Combined type ADHD which has characteristics of both.

Checklist of Inattention Symptoms

According to the DSM-5, inattention can be diagnosed if there are six or more characteristic symptoms in children up to the age of 16 or five or more symptoms for adolescents 17 and older, as follows:

- Often fails to pay attention to details or makes careless mistakes in schoolwork or other activities
- Often has trouble holding attention on tasks or play activities
- Often does not seem to listen when spoken to directly
- Often does not follow through on instructions or fails to finish schoolwork or chores
- Often has trouble organizing tasks and activities.
- Often avoids, dislikes, or is reluctant to do tasks that require mental effort over a long period of time
- Often loses things needed to complete tasks or activities
- Is easily distracted
- Is often forgetful in daily activities.

Checklist for Hyperactivity Symptoms

According to the DSM-5, hyperactivity and impulsivity can be diagnosed if there are six or more symptoms in children up to the age of 16 or five or more symptoms for adolescents 17 and older, as follows:

- Often fidgets with the hands or feet or squirms whenever seated

- Often leaves his or her seat despite being told sit still
- Often runs or climbs in situations where it is not appropriate
- Often unable to play or take part in leisure activities quietly
- Is often "on the go" as if unnaturally driven
- Often talks excessively
- Often blurts out an answer before a question has been completed
- Often has trouble waiting for his or her turn
- Often interrupts or intrudes on other's conversations or activities

Completing the Diagnosis

In order for ADHD to be definitely definitively diagnosis, the symptoms must meet four key criteria outlined in the DSM-5:

- The inattentive or hyperactive-impulsive symptoms must have been present before the age of 12.
- The symptoms must be present in two or more settings, such as at home, with friends, or in school.
- The symptoms must interfere with or reduce the quality of the child's ability to function at school, in social situations, or when performing normal, everyday tasks
- The symptoms cannot be explained any other mental condition (such as a mood disorder) or occur as part of a schizophrenic or psychotic episode.

Diagnosing ADHD in Children and Adults

The most commonly used and recommended test for evaluating a child or adult for ADHD is a standard assessment that is designed to identify behavioral patterns and traits associated with ADHD.

If your child is between age 4 and 18 and you suspect he or she may have ADHD, the American Academy of Pediatrics recommends that your child's primary doctor/pediatrician do the initial behavioral screening evaluation. During an office visit, the doctor will meet with your child and you and ask a series of questions to determine if your child shows persistent signs of inattention and/or impulsivity and hyperactivity and whether they occur in more than one situation, such as at home and in school.

If your child's pediatrician suspects ADHD, he will likely recommend a formal evaluation by a mental health professional such as neurologist or psychologist who can do neuropsychological testing. This type of testing goes more in-depth than the standard screening. This testing will include screening for auditory and visual processing and sensory development, among other things. The idea is that by identifying the contributing factors of ADHD, the doctor can recommend a treatment approach that addresses the underlying cause(s) as well as the ADHD.

If a doctor is having difficulty pinning down the diagnosis, she may recommend neurological imaging. A SPECT (single photon emission computed tomography) scan measures blood flow in the brain. A radioactive dye is injected in the arm, and a series of pictures are taken of the head. These are turned into 3-D images and screened to see where the brain appears more and less active. Children diagnosed under age 6 were much more likely to have had neurological imaging compared to those 6 and older (41.8 % versus 25 %).

Adults, meanwhile, are initially screened using the Adult ADHD Self-Report Scale.

This test cannot diagnose ADHD. The series of questions is intended to identify whether a more formal evaluation with a neurologist or psychologist should be considered.

Parents With ADHD Raising Children with ADHD

ADHD runs in families. That means that a child with ADHD is likely to have a mom or dad with the same disorder. It's critically important that the parent -- as well as the child -- be diagnosed and treated.

Why Parenting Is So Tough When You and Your Child Have ADHD

Parenting a child, any child, is a difficult task, to begin with. When you have a child with ADHD you are parenting a child who has greater demands, needs more involvement, and requires greater patience and understanding by the parent.

Add to the mix additional siblings of the ADHD child and conflicts, attention pulled in different directions, feelings of resentment by the child who requires less attention all these factors combine to create a parenting role that can quickly become overwhelming.

When a parent has undiagnosed ADHD, the difficulty level is ratcheted up even higher. If an ADHD parent's child also has ADHD, there can often be significant dysfunction within the family. A parent with untreated ADHD will certainly have a hard time following through with treatment recommendations for the child keeping track of a child's prescription, filling the prescription, administering the child's medication on a regular schedule, keeping track of when the prescription needs refilling, creating routines and structure at home, implementing and following through with behavioral or reward programs at home, etc.

If a parent has ADHD, that parent may also have a very difficult time being consistent with their child. Parenting skills will be affected by the parent's own ADHD. Studies show that parents with ADHD tend to provide less supervision, have more difficulty keeping tabs on their children and knowing where they are and are less adept at creative problem-solving.

If an issue or problem comes up, parents with ADHD tend to address it the same way again and again rather than thinking of other ways to handle the situation more effectively. It is often difficult for those with ADHD to be flexible in their approaches to parenting.

Identifying and Treating Adult ADHD

In the past, ADHD was mainly considered an academic or school issue for children. ADHD, however, is a 24 hour a day condition. It not only impairs school or work functioning, it also can have a significant impact on families and social relationships. There is even a high incidence of divorce in families in which a member has ADHD.

When a child is first diagnosed with ADHD, it is important to also screen the rest of the family to determine whether additional family members have ADHD. Once family members with ADHD are diagnosed, treatment can begin -- and other family members can begin to make sense of the challenges they've been encountering. By properly identifying ADHD in individuals, treatment can be so much more effective and family life much more joyful.

Treating ADHD

ADHD is typically treated from a number of angles. Medications, such as ritalin, are used to increase attention. Behavioral therapy interventions are used to condition behaviors conducive to better relationships, learning opportunities, and discipline. And mindfulness is taught to help sufferers of ADHD learn to concentrate for extended periods of time.

Traditional treatment of ADHD is far from perfect. Ritalin can come with significant side effects, and behavioral interventions are hard to implement outside the therapist's room. For this reason, researchers are still looking for alternatives, and CBD has come under the microscope

Medications used for ADHD

Two types of drugs are approved to treat ADHD: stimulants and non-stimulants.

- Stimulants. Stimulant drugs are the most commonly used medications to treat ADHD. Stimulants work by increasing brain chemicals, including dopamine, that are critical for transmitting messages between brain neurons. In kids, 70 to 80 percent show improvement in symptoms within one to two hours of taking the medication. In adults, 70 percent report noticeable improvement from stimulants within hours of using the medication.

  The two generic stimulants, also known as central nervous system stimulants, that are widely used to treat ADHD are methylphenidate (Concerta, Aptensio XR) and dextro-amphetamine (Adderall).

- Non-stimulants. In cases where a stimulant drug is not well tolerated or preferred, there is atomoexetine (Straterra), a non-stimulant that helps increase a brain chemical called norepinephrine. This chemical can help improve focus, while tamping down impulsiveness and hyperactivity. Clonidine (Kapvay) and Guanfacine

(Intuniv) are also non-stimulants and work slightly differently to achieve similar effects.

Therapy

Cognitive behavioral therapy and psychoeduation are recommended for people with ADHD to provide a framework for how to better manage emotions and general behavior. Therapy can also focus on strategies to help with self- regulation and self-monitoring. This education can help a child or adult with ADHD as they face day-to-day challenge's at home, in the classroom, at work, and in social situations. In addition, social skills groups can be beneficial for children and teens with ADHD, who often struggle with their social interactions, due to impulsivity. Therapy usually occurs one time per week, for 45 minutes at a time.

A therapist may also recommend alternative therapies and/or dietary changes that have proven helpful with managing different symptoms of ADHD. These may include:

- Meditation and mindfulness exercises to address the anxiety so often associated with ADHD.
- Working with an ADHD coach to learn organizational techniques and other day-to-day coping skills.
- Emotional freedom technique (EFT). Also known as tapping, EFT involves using the fingers to tap on a series of meridians on the body that can activate emotional release and healing.

- neurofeedback training (or EEG biofeedback) is utilized in an attempt to teach/train one who struggles with ADHD to produce the brain wave patterns associated with focus.
- Dietary improvements that focus on eating foods that reduce inflammation in the body, which in turn can help the brain function more optimally. This includes limiting white flour, white sugar, processed foods, and incorporating more fruits and vegetables, as well as omega-3 fatty acid rich foods such as walnuts and salmon.

Tips to decrease side effects

Stomach upsets, weight loss, insomnia are all common side effects of ADHD medications. Often they are mild, not lasting beyond the first few weeks but not always. For many kids, the battle with side effects is constant.

ADHD medications are extremely beneficial for the vast majority of kids, but most will have one or more side effects,".

Whether you will then switch to a different medication will depend on the benefits and how significant the side effects are. If the medication is helping the ADHD symptoms, sometimes it's worth it to tough it out and see if the side effects go away, which they often do. Other times you can work around the side effects, such as giving the medication with food to avoid stomachaches. But sometimes the side effects prove unacceptable and a change of medication is required,".

Stomach and Appetite Troubles

Stomach upsets often disappear within a few weeks, as the child's system gets used to the ADHD medication. Many children, however, continue to have appetite problems. Try these three simple steps:

- Give ADHD medication with food. If morning medication is taken after breakfast, there's less risk of stomach upsets.
- Encourage healthy snacking. Have lots of healthy after-school and bedtime snacks available. High-protein and energy bars, protein shakes, and liquid meals such as Carnation Instant Breakfast and Ensure are good options.
- Change dinnertime. Eat later in the evening, when your child's medication has worn off.

Headaches

Headaches, like stomach upsets, are related to taking ADHD medication without food in the stomach. "It's like having a strong cup of coffee on an empty stomach." Try these tips:

- Always give ADHD medication with food. Without food, ADHD medication gets absorbed more quickly, which causes blood levels of the medication to rise quickly. This can trigger a headache.
- Consider long-acting medication. Headache can also be a rebound effect when medication is wearing off

quickly, and is more common with short-acting medications. It may be necessary to switch to a longer-acting version of the drug or try a different ADHD medication altogether.

Difficulty Sleeping

Sleep problems are common for children with ADHD, partly because of the child's naturally high activity level. For many kids, insomnia occurs when a stimulant medication wears off. For others, the stimulant affects them much like coffee affects adults.

To offset sleep problems, it helps to develop a bedtime ritual for the child. This routine will help the child calm down at bedtime and get the sleep they need. Try these tips:

- Give the morning dose of ADHD medication earlier in the day.
- Discuss medication changes with the doctor. It may be necessary to try shorter-acting medications.
- Don't allow your child to drink caffeinated beverages. Cocoa and many sodas, coffees, and teas all contain caffeine. A child who drinks these in the afternoon or evening may be tossing and turning at bedtime.
- Establish a sleep-only zone. Your child's bedroom should be dedicated to sleep -- not for homework, not for entertainment. Move the computer, radio, television, toys, and games to another room. A few

stuffed animals are fine, but there should be no other distractions.

- Teach your child to relax at bedtime. A special blanket or a stuffed animal can help a child fall asleep. But it's best to avoid bedtime activities that depend on a parent's presence -- like rocking or holding the child until sleep comes.
- Establish consistency. Bedtimes and waking times should be the same seven days a week. Waking times are more important than bedtimes in establishing sleep rhythms. It is easier to enforce a waking time than a bedtime. "Sleeping in" can be a sign that the child is not getting enough sleep.
- Establish daytime routines. Regular meal and activity times help, too. Routines make it easier for children to "wind down" to sleep.
- Discourage midnight visits. Waking up at night can become a habit for children. It can also be a way to get attention. While you don't want to let a child cry themselves to sleep, it's best to discourage middle-of-the-night visits with mom and dad or midnight snacks. Also, don't allow interesting toys near the child's bed (a stuffed animal or two is fine).
- Avoid sleep medications. Medications stop working over time, and may affect daytime alertness. They may also wear off during the night, and cause night waking. Some medications may cause nightmares or other types of sleep problems. If medications are absolutely necessary, talk to your child's doctor about safe and effective treatments.

- Consider medical problems. Allergies, asthma, or conditions that cause pain can disrupt sleep. If your child snores loudly and/or pauses in breathing, medical evaluation is necessary. Consult your physician for help with the possible medical causes of sleep problems.

Tics

Tics are involuntary motor movements such as excessive eye blinking, throat clearing, sniffing, blinking, shrugging, or head-turning. About one in three boys and one in six girls with ADHD will develop tics with or without medication. "ADHD medications can bring out an underlying predisposition to tics but the medications don't cause tics,".

Chart your child's unusual movements. Talk to your pediatrician if you think your child may have tics. A change in medication, or combining medications, may help.

Growth Problems

Some children taking stimulant ADHD medications lose their appetite, which in turn can affect weight and growth. Most children may have a tendency not to gain weight over the first six to nine months of treatment, but then resume normal weight. Over two years, the majority of children weigh three to five pounds less than they would if not on medications -- and might be 0.1 to 0.5 inches shorter than their peers.

"A very small group of children is very sensitive to these medications,". "They lose their appetite, which means they lose a significant amount of weight -- so they don't grow." The ADHD medication by itself does not stunt growth. Rather, the child doesn't eat enough to get necessary nutrition for growth. Try these tips:

- Plot a growth chart. Make sure the pediatrician takes height and weight prior to starting ADHD drugs. Measurements should be made and charted three to four times a year.
- Encourage snacking. If your child has lost weight, encourage snacking on high-protein nutrition bars, protein shakes, and liquid meals such as Carnation Instant Breakfast and Ensure.
- Studies show that most kids will catch up in height and weight. "ADHD kids are often a couple of years behind other kids in growth maturation and puberty, so parents tend to worry about them,". "Puberty will just come later, probably at 15 rather than 13. By puberty, almost all kids have caught up to the normal height and weight they would have had if they had not been taking the medications."

Noticeable Mood Changes

For many kids, ADHD medications bring a sunnier mood and more enjoyment in life. But occasionally, a child becomes too quiet and seems sadder, depressed, moody an extreme emotional change. Such emotional changes could prove to be an unacceptable side effect or perhaps a sign that the dose of medication is too high. If the moodiness is especially noticeable when the medication is wearing off, it could be a sign of what's known as "rebound effect," and may require a change in ADHD medication.

"The medication may be making the kid irritable, as happens more often with younger kids," says Parker. "But if the child is feeling sad, depressed, or extremely irritable and the mood doesn't lift in a week or two that might not be something you can work around. The cure should never be worse than the disease, so it may be a sign to change the medication." Try this tip:

- Chart your child's mood changes. Note your child's highs and lows, and the time of day they occur. Then talk to the pediatrician

Rebound of Difficult Behaviors

Often the ADHD symptoms are under control early in the day, when the blood has a high level of medication. As the medicine wears off and leaves the body, there may be a rebound effect. The difficult behaviors may return, often worse than before. This is not a true side effect, but rather a result of medication wearing off. If your child has afternoon irritability and trouble concentrating, it could be a sign of rebound effect. Try these tips:

- Chart your child's behavior. Note the time of day that behaviors change, and what's happening.

- Talk to the doctor. If there seems to be a pattern of ADHD symptoms appearing in the afternoon or evening, the child may need another short-acting medication in the afternoon. Or the child may need a different combination of medications, including a nonstimulant or low-dose tricyclic antidepressant.

Dizziness

Dizziness can occur when the ADHD medication dose is too high. If you notice your child gets dizzy, have your child drink fluids and get your child's blood pressure checked right away. If that's normal, try this tip:

- Talk to the doctor. It may be time to switch to an extended-release medication to smooth out the highs and lows in medication levels in the blood.

Nausea, Tiredness

With the nonstimulant drug Strattera, nausea and excessive tiredness are common side effects in the first few weeks. To help the child build up a tolerance to the medication, try these tips:

- Start with a low dose. Increase the dose by a small amount every one to two weeks.
- Change dosing. Give the dose at night or divide the dose into morning and late afternoon dosages

In September 2005 the FDA issued a public health advisory about rare reports of suicidal thinking in children and adolescents taking Strattera. Strattera has been associated with an increased risk of suicidal thinking in children and adolescents with ADHD. Youth who start this drug require close monitoring for suicidal thinking or unusual changes in behavior for the first few months or after the dosage is changed.

Increased Heart Rate & Pulse

These side effects develop when a child takes an ADHD drug plus a decongestant like Sudafed. "You're mixing two potent stimulants together,". "That's when we get a call that a kid is getting panicky at school only to find out the parents gave him cold medicine that morning." In fact, pseudoephedrine (Sudafed) dramatically increases all side effects from stimulants. Try these tips:

- Use a nasal spray when your child has a cold.
- Skip the ADHD medication when your child is stuffed up and needs a decongestant.
- Or, choose a cold medicine that doesn't contain pseudoephedrine.

Other Mental Health Conditions Associated with ADHD

There are several conditions that are associated with ADHD, including anxiety, learning disabilities, oppositional defiant disorder, substance abuse, biopolar disorder,25 depression, and social anxiety. This is why it's critical that an ADHD evaluation also include an initial assessment for these related conditions, as well as ongoing screenings if an ADHD diagnosis is made. If one of these related conditions is also diagnosed, the doctor can recommend a number of treatments options that, similar to ADHD, will include medication and therapy.

Living with ADHD

A child or adult diagnosed with ADHD faces daily challenges that impact nearly every area of his or her life. But persistence in finding the right medication and dosage while also making time for therapy that focuses on effective behavioral coping techniques will be the key to successfully managing this condition.

CBD Oil

Cannabidiol, or CBD, is one of the active cannabinoids in cannabis. It can actually account for up to 40% of the active cannabinoid content.

CBD hemp oil is made from hemp that has high amounts of CBD and low amounts of THC. THC is the cannabinoid that most people are familiar with. It is responsible for the "high" that you get if you take or smoke marijuana.

This means that CBD oil is non-psychoactive. This has allowed CBD oil to be used for a lot of medical purposes because you don't have to worry about it affecting your mental state.

I don't know about you, but even if something was really helpful, I wouldn't be able to function at all if I was stoned all day and night.

CBD Oil Dosage

we've got the dosage topic covered but you should always consult with your doctor before beginning any form of treatment. CBD-rich oil comes in a variety of concentrations and forms, and while most bottles come with a user manual, CBD oil works differently for each person. If you've never tried CBD or you are still trying to figure out what works best for you, then continue reading as there are a few important things to understand about CBD oil and CBD oil dosages.

Important Things to Know About CBD Oil Dosages

1) Every Person is Different and May Require a Different Dosage

If you've been following the articles on our site, then you have probably heard of the endocannabinoid system. This is a unique system in our body that's responsible for improving and maintaining our mental and physical health. CBD is believed to help regulate that system by binding with various receptors located within cell and tissue systems. Those receptors are referred to as CB1 and CB2.

The endocannabinoid system is extremely complex and far from understood, leaving researchers trying to determine whether or not the CBD directly or indirectly effects those receptors, and exactly what role they play in affecting ones' health.

While the exact way they effect our system still remains a mystery to most researchers, what we do know is that every person has a different endocannabinoid system, and therefore while the instructions on a CBD oils' bottle may be informative and clear, the standard dosing may affect two different people in completely different ways.

2) Genetics, Tolerance and General Health

If you accept the fact that everyone is different, then you can understand that everyone has his/her own genetics, tolerance, and general health. There are those that suffer from severe debilitating conditions and others that are only looking to cure their day to day anxiety. Each person has their own reasons for wanting to take CBD oil, and it's assumed that all of these factors – genetics, tolerance and general health – will come into play as far as how well CBD works for them. It cannot be expected that someone who is in the prime of their game, from a health perspective, will require the same dosage as someone who has severe medical issues.

3) It's Not a Miracle Cure

Regardless of whether the right dosage of CBD will work for your body or not, it's important to understand that CBD oil is not a miracle cure. Don't expect to take a few drops and, Voilà, you're cured. The effects of CBD oil are not instant, and people constantly make the same mistake – they use CBD for a short period, expecting it to cure them instantly, and when it doesn't work they complain and ask for a refund. CBD can take time to work and similar to your health issues, it won't happen overnight. The key is finding the right dosage.

The Standard CBD Oil Dosage Manual

Now, remember, this guide is a general one, and it is extremely important to read the dosage instructions on the CBD oil you are taking, especially as results from certain dosages may affect you differently then others. Furthermore, it is always best to contact the CBD oil company to ask them the right dosage for your medical condition and consult with your doctor if required. With that said, there are a few common dosage strategies that might work for you:

Start by taking one drop on the first day. It's important to see how you feel as everyone reacts differently. It may even cause you irritation, and therefore it's important to stop.

If all goes well, increase the amount to 2 drops per day for the first 3-4 weeks. This is the testing period to see if it is helping any of your symptoms.

Spread the drops throughout the day. For example, take one in the morning and one in the evening.

If you don't experience any change, then increase at a slow rate and see how you feel. With each person, it is a question of finding the right dosage.

Remember that many CBD oil companies advise you to put the drops under your tongue and let them take effect for at least 30 seconds.

Numerous sites state the following dosage guidelines when using CBD orally:

- General Health: 2.5-15mg CBD
- Chronic pain: 2.5-20 mg CBD
- Sleep disorders: 40-160 mg CBD

CBD Effects and CBD Benefits

CBD oil effects your body by binding to cannabinoid receptors. You have cannabinoid receptors all over your body, including your skin and digestive tract.

CBD oil can also act as a 5-HT1 receptor agonist, meaning it can help with depression and anxiety by playing in a role in the serotonin pathways.

Because CBD oil affects so many aspects of your body, including the endocannabinoid system, it can help with inflammation, mood, memory, immune system, reproduction, pain perception, sleep, and appetite.

The biggest benefits, and why it has gotten so much of the spotlight lately, is that CBD oil has helped people with rare conditions such as Dravet syndrome, a rare form of epilepsy that is hard to treat. People have gone from having multiple seizures per day to being seizure free for an entire week using CBD oil.

One strain of cannabis is called Charlotte's Web, which has almost no THC in it, and has been used for medical purposes ever since it helped a girl named Charlotte stop having really bad seizures after trying all the other approaches.

CBD oil has clearly proven itself as a therapeutic substance to help a variety of ailments, and it can also play a role in helping anxiety and depression.

CBD Oil Side Effects

CBD oil can inhibit hepatic drug metabolism and activity of some liver enzymes, such as cytochrome P450.

One side effect from taking CBD oil can be having a "dry mouth", which if you have ever smoked marijuana, you know what this feels like.

At the current moment, it is unclear as to whether or not it positively or negatively affects people with Parkinson's disease.

However, most studies conducted on CBD oil have shown little to no side effects. This specific review shows that controlled use is safe and non-toxic for humans.

I didn't experience any side effects when I experimented with CBD oil that had no THC in it.

My Personal Experiment and Findings Using CBD Oil

Here is where CBD oil can get tricky. When I began my journey into supplementing with CBD to see its potential, I ran into a lot of companies where I had no idea what I was getting.

The quality matters, as it would be easy to market something as CBD oil when it has very little CBD in it at all.

Some of the products I tried I felt nothing at all even at high doses, others had weird ingredients, and it wasn't until I started experimenting with prescription CBD and high quality brands that I started to see benefits from it.

I noticed a slight decrease in anxiety and it helped to ease some of my digestive symptoms. When I took a large amount of the tincture as an experiment it had a significant calming effect.

CBD Tincture, CBD Capsules, & CBD Vape

I tried a tincture, capsules, spray, and a vape. Each of which were different brands.

Depending on how often you want to take it, capsules were by far the easiest method and also the most expensive. With capsules you know exactly how much you are getting each time and it is easy to carry with you if you want to keep dosing throughout the day every few hours or so.

The tincture you would have to carry around and depending on the quality of the cap, it could leak out into your pocket. The tincture would be harder to dose with throughout the day and the dosing wouldn't be as accurate.

The spray was very easy to use and would be a bit easier to carry around than a tincture, but could still pose problems if you kept it in your pocket because you could accidentally spray some inside your pants.

The vape would be very easy to carry around, but I don't really enjoy having to inhale something, as it reminds me of when I had a problem with drugs back in the day. You'd also have to use it more often. This could be a great method for you, however, the brand I used was probably low quality and I have no idea if using a better brand would change my opinion on using a vape.

CBD versus CBD Combined with THC

THC and CBD have a synergistic effect, meaning that they both enhance each other's beneficial properties. Many people believe that it is optimal to take both at the same time.

I am in a state where medical marijuana is legal. I called up a doctor and received my prescription really easily. I used the network that they recommended and got both a spray with very low THC in it and a spray with a slightly higher concentration of THC.

I was told to take two sprays of the low THC concentration every 4 hours throughout the day and then two sprays of the higher THC concentration after dinner and at night as needed to help with sleep.

I noticed after a few days that the higher concentration of THC was actually making my sleep worse and I started to have weird nightmares. I started to lose some motivation and overall didn't like the feeling at all, so I stopped taking it.

Again, with all things, each person will react differently so you will have to know yourself well and maybe experiment with a few different concentrations to know what is right for you. My friend used an equal ratio of CBD to THC and after just a week, his blood pressure was down, his bowel movements were much more regular, and it helped with his lactose intolerance.

Where To Find CBD Oil For Sale

Of all the different brands and products that I tried, the best (and most expensive) was the one that came from the Statewide Collective in California. With them you an get the exact ratio you want, they only have good ingredients, and it delivers right to your door. The best option will most likely be to get CBD oil that comes from medically grown cannabis plants and a controlled process.

The second best option was Elixinol. They also only use good ingredients, have actually had their products tested so you know what you are getting, and I felt beneficial effects from it. Their farmers are 4th generation hemp farmers in Europe.

The rest I got varying results from. The random tinctures I bought at local head shops had unknown effects. It would be hard to know what you are getting if you just drive down and buy the first brand you see.

I wouldn't particularly recommend ordering from Organabus, as I didn't feel anything from their vape product and didn't have any results with anything else on their site. Their site was also a bit confusing and I was unsure of what I was ordering. However, their customer support was great over email.

The others had some interesting ingredients and although not particularly harmful, I like to take only the purest and highest quality ingredients. If you are already purchasing something for its beneficial effects, why waste your money by trying to buy a cheaper product when it doesn't work for the thing you are trying to do in the first place.

Using The Vape Pen

Where to Buy CBD Oil and How To Get a Prescription

If you are looking to take CBD oil with THC to combine both of their beneficial effects or you want the highest quality you can get, if you live in an area where it is legal you can either just buy it from local vendors or get a prescription very easily.

I made a costly mistake of going to a "doctor" that my friend swore by who would prescribe me the "right concoctions" for what I needed. In the end, I wasted $300 for someone to not even listen to my health problems and just assure me that I needed marijuana and gave me a prescription.

If you live in an area where you can get a prescription, it is much faster and more cost effective to get on Skype with a doctor for 10 minutes and get your prescription within the hour. One such place is Hello MD but I've heard of others that are extremely easy. My friend got on Skype and got his prescription in 45 minutes and I think only paid $40.

In the state of California, once you have your prescription you can order the best products from the places that you need a prescription. One that I used is www.statewidecollective.org.

If you don't live in a place where you can get a prescription (or even if you can get a prescription), Elixinol was the best brand that I found that anyone can order from and be able to benefit from CBD oil. They offer capsules, sprays, etc.

Conclusion

CBD oil is virtually a risk free way to potentially help you with health problems like digestive issues and things such as anxiety and depression. If you suffer from insomnia, anxiety, or stress I would order some CBD oil and see if it works for you.

CBD Oil for ADHD

If you or someone you love suffers from ADHD (Attention Deficit/Hyperactivity Disorder), you've probably spent what feels like a lifetime searching for a treatment that reduces the symptoms without all the negative side effects. Now, you can stop looking. CBD oil might be just the solution you've been hoping for. If you're curious about using CBD oil for ADHD, you've come to the right place.

Attention Deficit Hyperactivity Disorder denoted by ADHD is a childhood disease that often continues until adulthood. Similarly, ADD is known as Attention Deficit Disorder that is an old name for ADHD.

These are anxiety-related disorders associated with distractibility and difficulties with attention, focus, and concentration. The only difference between ADHD and ADD is that ADHD is linked to hypersensitivity whereas ADD is not.

These behavior-related disorders associate with chemicals imbalance in the brain such as low levels of dopamine. ADHD/ADD usually gets treated with medications like Adderall and Ritalin both of which leads to severe side effects including, muscle twitches, increased heart rate, tremors, anxiety, hallucinations, psychosis, and much more.

Fortunately, there are some alternative treatments available that are getting accepted within the medical community.

One of such procedures includes CBD oil that helps in maintaining the dopamine levels and creates a level of calm. Also, doctors are voicing support for managing ADHD or ADD from cannabis.

Research backs this up

While there is not a ton of research into CBD oil as a treatment for ADHD, the studies done thus far have been promising. Since CBD also has the effects of improving mood and decreasing anxiety, which are often present in sufferers of ADHD, it is likely to have positive results even if it does not affect the underlying disorder.

More research is necessary to determine whether CBD will become a mainstream treatment for ADHD. Controlled studies should be conducted in the near future, due to the medical field's current interest in CBD, as well as increasing legality making such studies possible.

.

Can CBD Oil Cure Your ADHD

The short answer to this question is no. (Sorry.) CBD oil relieves the symptoms of ADHD, not the underlying cause. It's very much like taking an aspirin to relieve your back pain. The aspirin just numbs the pain for a while. If you stop taking the aspirin, the pain will return because the original problem (pulled muscle, bulging disc) is still there.

CBD oil makes it easier for your brain to "level out" and run more smoothly. That means less distraction and more focus. But if you stop taking CBD oil or the CBD oil you took wears off, your brain will revert to its original mode of operation (e.g., chemical imbalance that leads to anxiety), and the ADHD symptoms will return.

That means that once you start taking CBD oil, you may need to continue taking it indefinitely. Don't read into that statement and assume that CBD is addictive—it's not. But if you want to live your life without ADHD symptoms, you'll have to keep taking CBD in one form or another. You can always choose to stop, and you'll feel no ill effects other than a return of your ADHD problems.

That may seem like a bleak outlook, but many who suffer from ADHD already deal with taking medications of one sort or another for the rest of their lives. And most of these medications have significant side effects that make them worse than the ADHD itself. How does CBD compare to those other medications in terms of side effects? That's the focus of our next section.

Does CBD Oil Get You High

There's good news for those of you worried about taking CBD oil for ADHD: you won't have to contend with couch lock, altered perceptions, lethargy, and the other "negative" effects of high-THC strains. That's because CBD and CBD oil doesn't get you high.

CBD products will not cause psychedelic effects because they have been produced in such a way so as to minimize THC count. In fact, CBD itself is what's known as an antagonist to THC, which means that CBD reduces just how high you can get.

How CBD Oil Works

The CBD in CBD oil works like a key in a lock. In this case, the locks are the millions of receptors in your brain. When the locks are closed, the receptors are inactive. But when the locks are open, the receptors are active. For ADHD, it's these active receptors that we're most concerned about because they are the source of the problem.

More specifically, we're concerned about the adenosine receptors that are largely responsible for reducing anxiety. For those without ADHD, the body does a pretty good job of controlling anxiety. But sometimes, the receptors don't fire on all cylinders, so to speak, or your brain doesn't produce enough of the chemical "keys" to keep the receptors active. When that happens, you can start to feel anxious, paranoid, and depressed—all major components of ADHD.

Cannabidiol, reported by people, helps in balancing the levels of dopamine in the brain. Dopamine is an essential neurotransmitter that regulates most of the cognitive processes including memory, moods, and attention. The deficiency of dopamine levels is one of the causes of ADHD.

The medication treatment for ADHD is designed to manage dopamine levels by stimulating its production and enhancing the ability of the patient to concentrate but, these medications cause serious side effects and withdrawal symptoms.

However, CBD oil showed a positive impact on patients without any side effects. It efficiently activates the anti-inflammatory, anti-anxiety, and anti-depressant receptors in the brain that helps in managing the symptoms.

ADHD or ADD associate with endocannabinoid deficiency; hence, it regulates the endocannabinoid system and aids in sustaining calm level. The activation of receptors in the brain help in treating hyperactivity and impulsiveness and control mood, memory, appetite, pain, and attention.

In the pathology of ADD or ADHD, the mechanism of cannabinoids is still unknown; however, it enhances the transmission of dopamine.

According to various studies, CBD increases concentration and ability to focus in ADHD patients by activating the adenosine receptors in the brain and even reduces anxiety. CBD oil manages the chemical imbalances in the brain and enables to work smoothly and halt distraction or hyperactivity.

The interesting characteristic of CBD is that it can act as the key that opens the lock to the adenosine receptors. When CBD is present, it stimulates activity within your brain and has a twofold effect on your behavior:

- CBD decreases many of the negative symptoms of ADHD.
- CBD increases your ability to concentrate and focus on one specific task.

Does it work

There is some clinical evidence that CBD works as a treatment for ADHD. There is a lot of anecdotal evidence that implies as much. Unfortunately, for years researchers did not have carte blanche to investigate that anecdotal evidence further. However, with legal issues out of the way, the necessary research can finally be undertaken. It's likely they'll find what users have been saying for years: you can use CBD to treat ADHD. At the very least, it will not harm you.

How Do You Use CBD Oil For ADHD

You take CBD oil like a tincture: simply administer a few drops under your tongue and hold them there without swallowing. Honestly, this is probably the easiest way to take a cannabis product. It's very discreet and very quick.

The CBD oil is absorbed into your bloodstream through the sublingual artery in your lower jaw. From there, it travels quickly to your brain. Because of the speed with which this all occurs, you can feel the effects of CBD oil almost immediately.

Even though there are no major side effects of CBD oil for ADHD, we still recommend starting small with one or two drops and increasing slowly until you find the right dose. Talk to the budtenders at your local dispensary for advice on where to start.

Other Health Benefits Of CBD Oil

Oh, are there! CBD oil can:

- Fight cancer cells
- Reduce artery blockage
- Make it easier to sleep
- Suppress muscle spasms

- Prevent nervous system degeneration
- Reduce inflammation
- Reduce blood sugar levels
- Decrease pain
- Reduce nausea and vomiting

And that's just the tip of the CBD iceberg! Because CBD has a wide variety of significant beneficial effects, it can treat:

- Acne
- AIDS
- ALS
- Anorexia
- Atherosclerosis
- Arthritis
- Autism
- Back pain
- Bipolar disorder
- Cancer
- Endocrine disorders
- Fibromyalgia
- Glaucoma
- Multiple sclerosis (MS)
- OCD
- Parkinson's disease
- PTSD
- Stroke

And a whole lot more. It really is a wonder drug for the new millennium.

Alternative Methods For Getting CBD For ADHD

➢ Marijuana plant

We say that with an exclamation point because if there's one thing about the cannabis community, it's that they're extremely creative when it comes to finding ways to take their marijuana.

You've probably heard about the old tried-and-true method of smoking a joint, blunt, or bong. But if discretion is more your thing, you can also get your daily CBD through:

- Edibles
- Dissolvable strips
- Live resin
- Weed tea
- Vape pens
- Weed candy
- CBD cream

CBD Oil Side Effects

When compared with other ADHD medications, CBD oil has no real negative side effects. You won't feel hungover or "out of it." You won't have stomach problems or migraines. About the only thing you can expect to feel after taking CBD oil is dry mouth. Many people who take CBD oil for ADHD don't even consider this a side effect when compared to other prescription medications. Dry mouth is a small price to pay for fewer ADHD symptoms.

Another possible "side effect" of CBD products is that the CBD can interfere with your liver's ability to break down ingredients in other drugs. So, if you take a blood pressure medication and add CBD oil for ADHD to the mix, the CBD will render the blood pressure medication ineffective. Even if you're not taking other medications, be sure to talk to your doctor before trying CBD oil for ADHD.

Important Facts To Know About CBD Oil For ADD And ADHD

- CBD oil not only interacts with the endocannabinoid system, but it also binds with serotonin receptors, vanilloid receptors, and adenosine receptors that have a significant impact on stress and pain management, mood management, and sleep-wake cycles.
- CBD oil was classified as a nutritional supplement, but after recognizing many health benefits, it is considered as a medicine by the British government.
- ADHD causes disturbances in the sleep cycle; however, CBD oil works as a sedative that helps in treating insomnia.
- CBD oil is non-toxic; therefore, even excessive intake of CBD oil causes no severe side effects, and it is nearly impossible to overdose.
- CBD oil consists of a very minute amount of THC; therefore, it is safe and quite effective in treating depression, anxiety, paranoia, and stress without making you high.
- A study conducted in 2013, revealed that CBD oil helps in blocking the addictive impact of painkillers like morphine. It protects the body from dealing with any severe side effects.

What Research Says

CBD Oil For ADD And ADHDA clinical study conducted in 2014, by Dr. Eva Milz and Dr. Franjo Grotenhermen in Germany, presented CBD oil as a successful treatment for ADHD or ADD.

They examined 30 patients that could not respond to the medications prescribed for ADD such as Adderall or Ritalin.Later, they ingested CBD oil, and it helped them in improving concentration and sleep and diminished hyperactivity.

Journal of Substance Use and Misuse published a study in 2013, presented some patients suffering from ADHD and self-medicating with CBD oil. The patients reported a reduction in their impulsiveness and improvement in other symptoms. Also, their hyperactive behaviors were improved. This result helped various medical experts to suggest CBD oil for treating the hyperactive type of ADHD.

Also, a randomized control trial, conducted in London's King College proved that cannabis is a perfect way of treating the symptoms of ADHD or ADD. The patients reported development in cognitive performance. CBD oil not only improved hyperactivity but also showed improvement in inattention.

Therefore, it is effective in treating all three types of Attention deficit hyperactivity disorder. Patients showed recovery in emotional liability and consistent amelioration in their hyperactive behaviors.

Dosage Of CBD Oil For ADHD

CBD oil is available in various forms and concentrations, and every person reacts to it differently. Therefore, to be safe, it is excellent if you start with a small dose and increases it gradually.

There is a lot of confusion related to the accurate dosage of the CBD oil because of different standards. However, the recommended serving standard is 25 mg of CBD oil taken twice a day.

Start with tinctures consisting of about 1000mg of the cannabinoid extracts. Purchase a bottle comprising of 500 drops and each drop of about 2 mg. The recommended dosage for ADD and ADHD for children is ingesting 5 to 10 drops of CBD oil, three times a day and later increasing the dose by 25 mg after every three to four weeks until the symptoms start diminishing and you get the desired result.

Also, you can reduce your dose accordingly if you start feeling any worsening symptoms. However, right results are shown by taking 40 mg daily for three weeks. But patients with severe ADHD reported the need to take more than 100mg of CBD oil for per day.

Use CBD Oil For ADHD

If you are a beginner, it is easy if you start using CBD oil for ADD and ADHD in the form of tinctures. Directly dispense few drops of CBD oil under your tongue and hold it there for about 60 to 90 seconds without swallowing. You can drink it only if you are unable to tolerate its taste. It is the easiest way of ingesting CBD oil.

After a minute or two, the CBD oil gets diffused through the sublingual artery into the bloodstream. From the sublingual artery, it directly reaches to the brain and results in producing the effects immediately. Start ingesting few drops of CBD oil and gradually increase the dosage until you start attaining the desired result.

Interesting Reviews About CBD Oil For ADHD

Evin, 11 years old boy informed about his story related to his suffering from ADHD and intake of CBD oil. He declared that he felt irritated and annoyed all at the same time and used to hurt himself. His anger was uncontrollable, and then Evin started taking CBD oil for his Attention Deficit Hyperactivity Disorder. After ingesting CBD oil for a few days, he started feeling calm and relaxed and observed his arguments changing into proper conversations.

However, when he skipped his CBD oil intake, he noticed his head getting warm. He reported that CBD oil helped him efficiently in managing the symptoms of ADHD. Evin started feeling relaxed and observed that nothing wrong ruined his mood and he dealt with everything without getting frustrated.

Nova, a little boy, was diagnosed with ADHD. He started feeling extreme changes in his behavior and used to be angry all the time. He kept on fighting and having sick days. His mother tried to find every possible therapy that could treat Nova's disease since he was three years old.

Later, she discovered CBD oil and started giving it to her son daily. She surprisingly noticed changes in the behaviors of her son. Also, Nova felt calm and began asking his mother for his CBD oil dosage.

Tara Eveland shared her story and even of her son suffering from ADHD. She declared that she was unable to concentrate and focus on various tasks. Tara used to talk excessively.

She never got good grades in school because of lack of focus and attention and even had issues with recalling and remembering. Tara also faced trouble in sleeping. Later she started the intake of CBD oil and noticed no problems with sleep. Also, her memory improved and she was able to be attentive and focus on things.

Finding the Best CBD oil for ADHD

Finding the best CBD oil for ADD and ADHD in the market is quite a hard task and may require a lot of research. However, some of the factors make it easy for you to find the best CBD oil company available.

These factors include quick shipping and service, product quality, third-party testing, customer happiness, and quality control. You can get the purest forms of CBD oil from the following companies.

According to the Center for Disease Control, 11 percent of American children ages 4-17 have an attention disorder. Pharmaceuticals like Ritalin and Adderall are commonly prescribed to treat this ADHD. Some of the common side effects of these drugs include headaches, dizziness, blurred vision, irritability, agitation, and restless feelings. Did we just say feeling restless? That sounds a lot like hyperactivity itself. Despite the many well documented side effects of common ADHD treatments, mainstream medical treatment has failed to provide alternatives to hard amphetamines for ADHD treatment. While there have been believers in CBD for ADHD treatment for some time, in recent years more clinical research has been completed regarding CBD and anxiety disorders. Yes, you read that right...anxiety disorders. While traditionally called ADHD, attention deficit disorder and hyperactivity disorder are actually two closely related anxiety disorders. And anxiety disorders have a well documented record with CBD. Furthermore, many CBD products include herbs, vitamins and minerals that are known to enhance focus, dealing with one of the main symptoms of AD/HD. We've combed through all of the top producers of CBD products and created a ranking of the best CBD products for ADHD with the following metrics:

Range of Products Score (1/5)

- Beginner Dosage Score: the lowest dosage available in this brand's product
- Experienced Dosage Score: the highest dosage available in this brand's product
- Delivery Method Score: the number of distinct delivery methods of CBD oil products

Cannabinoid Variant Score (1/5)

- The range of documented cannabinoids in the brand's products. Often achieved through different distillation methods or extraction methods utilizing the whole hemp plant.

Product Purity Score (1/5)

- Measure of extraction method, whether a brand's products are certified organic, and quality control testing employed by each brand.

Sourcing Score (1/5)

- Measure of location hemp is sourced from as it relates to environmental toxins and greater cannabinoid density. Additionally, a measure of the number of chemicals used in the production of the hemp (if any).

- The brand's range of delivery methods that are particularly well suited for aiding the medical issue at hand. In the case of using CBD Oil for ADHD, tinctures and sublingual delivery methods are the most documented source of relief.

- The brand's range of additional herbs, vitamins, minerals, and carrier devices that are known to aid the medical issue at hand. In the case of ADHD, focus-specific botanicals may be added for enhanced affect. Additionally, many people with ADHD suffer from anxiety. We have also weighted anti-anxiety herbs for this reason.

Best CBD Oils for ADHD

1. ENDOCA

ENDOCA is a small-scale family-run CBD Oil sourced from Denmark, that focuses making on affordable CBD Oil products accessible to all. ENDOCA boasts a wide-range of therapeutic CBD products, optimal sourcing, Supercritical CO2 extraction, and 100% control over the entire manufacturing process. ENDOCA is one of the few companies to have been awarded the GMP certification. Northern Europe has one of the best sources for hemp as it is grown in an area with low levels of pollution. This is essential for hemp as it readily absorbs pollution. ENDOCA'S Tincture, Drops, Capsules, Suppositories, Ovules, Crystals, Salves, Body Butter, and Chewing Gum are all third-party tested which adds to overall quality control and integrity of the product. All raw materials are lab-tested by independent parties at multiple points to ensure purity. Those experiencing ADHD symptoms should try the ENDOCA tincture. Above all other forms of CBD delivery including the capsules, crystals, and suppositories, the tincture has proven the most affective against ADHD and ADHD-like symptoms. Beginner doses are available at 300 milligrams or 3% CBD upwards to 1500 milligrams or 15% CBD.

2. Green Roads World

Green Roads is an exceptional CBD oil that offers a wide range of CBD Oil products including tinctures, syrups, creams, capsules, edibles, and beverages. All products are compounded by a highly experienced and licensed pharmacist, and incorporate not only cannabinoids, but other therapeutic botanicals, such as menthol and melatonin. These compounds are third-party tested to ensure quality and purity. What's more the hemp is sourced in Europe in ideal climates then shipped to Green roads World headquartered in the United States. We like the full-spectrum CBD that includes CBD, CBG, CBN, and terpenes- all yielded through the most expensive and effective CO_2 extraction method. Green Roads have been featured on Forbes, Yahoo! Finance, NBC, HERB, HIGH TIMES, and ESPN. For those suffering with matters of attention and focus, the best delivery method with the greatest affects come sub lingually via tincture. Green Roads offers a wide range of tincture concentrations: 100mg, 250mg, 350mg, 550mg, 30 ml,1000mg, 1500mg. We understand that ADHD often is accompanied by other symptoms and we are excited to share that Green Roads offers Custom CBD Oil Formulations to help you treat symptoms of ADHD, Insomnia, and other related symptoms.

CBD Drip offers a full spectrum CBD oil that contains not only CBD, but all of the therapeutic cannabinoids of the plant- this is what you should expect from a quality CBD source. CBD Drip uses organic high quality European industrial hemp- one of the best regions for growing hemp due to low pollution levels. If you suffer from all matters of attention, all of CBD Drip's products are useful for focus. We highly recommend starting with a tincture and giving this product a month to build in your system for optimal results. Supplementing a dosage with a vape liquid is common though be sure to start small and build accordingly. For some brain-fog is an accompanying symptom to hyperactivity and lack of focus. If you feel groggy and foggy, you could try one of their vape pens for a more acute affect. Overall, their CBD tinctures are a versatile product reported to help with anxiety, pain, headaches, insomnia, seizures, and acne.

3. Bluebird Botanicals

Bluebird Botanicals uses top-quality hemp, sustainable and organically grown in Colorado. They offer an excellent selection of blends and dosages, and maintain ethical business practices. All their broad-spectrum hemp extract is third party tested for purity and quality. Bluebird uses both CO_2 and alcohol extraction practices when crafting their products. It's all in the name with Bluebird botanicals which includes additional botanical compounds with myriad therapeutic applications. The company offers discounts of 25- 40% to disabled, veteran, and low-income customers. Users with AD/HD may benefit from Bluebird's CBD concentrates, which are available in several doses and formulations. The "Signature" features hemp seed extract in hemp seed oil, a comprehensive blend of raw and heatd cannabinoids plus wildcrafted frankincense serratta CO_2 extract, and cold pressed black seed oil. We recommend this product in particular for individuals experiencing hyperactivity, attention deficits, and all matters related to focus. The added frankincense may help augment relief from AD/HD related problem.

4. Pure Hemp Botanicals

Pure Hemp Botanicals has earned a reputation for consistency in its CBD oil products, and transparency in its testing methods, with quality control measures that far exceed market standards. All plants are organically grown, processed, and packaged in Colorado. To ensure that the help extract is pure and potent, products are lab tested, labeled by batch with all lab test results posted directly to their website. Of their many CBD oil products, we recommend tinctures for all ADD ADHD related symptoms.

Tinctures are an infusion of organic hemp seed oil with full spectrum hemp extract, and when taken over time will build in your system for long-lasting affects. When experiencing brain fog or focus issues, you could try a vape pen for accute relief, though it should be known that most of the data points towards tinctures exclusively for AD/HD Tinctures are available in concentrations of 300 mg, 750 mg, 1500 mg, or 3000 mg of cannabinoid extract per package. The general rule is to start small and build over time- understanding that each individual's body chemistry requires a slightly different dosage.

5. 4 Corners Cannabis

4 Corners Cannabis offers CBD from a single propietary strain grown organically in Durango, Colorado. As the makers of the products are also the growers, they have total control over the process from the "soil to the oil." The owners collectively have devoted over 20,000 hours to crafting the finest CBD products and are well-versed in the differences between low quality and high quality CBD oils- and especially genetics. This strain is grown as 6,900 feet of elevation- making for a more pure, and far less polluted product. In 4 Corners products you will not only find the CBD but also the the CBC CBE, and CBL. This is the "entourage effect" and why when dosing this product, you can dose much lower than other products. For anyone who struggles with ADD and ADHD symptoms you don't need much of 4 Corners hemp extract. Their CBD tinctures come in three distinct concentrations: 250 milligrams, 500 milligrams, and 1000 milligrams. Be sure to take the tincture daily and start with small doses as this product will build in your system over time. If

you're not getting the desired effect, you can take more without concerns of side effects.

6. Green Gorilla

Green Gorilla is an international group that sources their hemp plants and CBD worldwide. They use certified organic and Non-GMO hemp that is third-party tested for purity and quality. All products are food grade and use olive oil as the carrier oil for their CBD which is 99% pure. Their Hemp & Olive product line offers a wide range of uses from supplemental health care to cosmetic care to pet care. We understand that ADHD is commonly treated with some potent drugs that have some scary side-effects- side-effects that are often times worse than lose of focus. We are pleased to find products that hold so much integrity, and help you focus without any come down. The World Health Organization has found no abuse potential or adverse health outcomes from pure CBD products. To deal with matters of attention, there is always an alternative. If you are suffering from ADHE try their Hemp and Olive Pure CBD oil line. Their oils com in three concentrations and contain no THC. For extreme hyper activity we recommend trying their pure CBD oil product available in a concentration of 7500 mg.

7. Elixinol

Colorado-based hemp and CBD oil company, Elixinol aims for high quality products. They achieve this though the use of organically sourced high-quality strains grown by industrial hemp farmers in Europe, the U.S. and Australia. They use a CO_2 cold extraction that preserves all of the cannabinoids and other therapeutic properties. Elixinol subjects all its CBD extracts to rigorous in-house testing, as well as additional third-party testing to ensure purity, absence of unwanted chemicals, and dosage accuracy. Elixinol has been featured on National Geographic, The Wall Street Journal, NBC, Men's Health and others. When it comes to ADHD the most recommended product for treatment of all related symptoms is a tincture. One of the most frequently asked questions is with regards to dosing. We recommend starting with a small dose and working up as needed. The tincture does not have acute affects. If you are looking for fast relief, you could try a vape liquid, though limited studies have been done to show the efficacy of a vape liquid on ADD and ADHD. This is why we recommend starting with a tincture and allowing that tincture to build over time in your system. Products are offered in either natural or cinnamon flavors. Beginners should start with the 300 mg concentration.

We'll also discuss the other health benefits of CBD oil and learn about alternative methods for getting CBD for ADHD. We know your attention span is short—Squirrel!—ours is too, so let's start at the beginning.

Final Thoughts

CBD oil really is one of the miracle oils from the nature due to the numerous effects it offer in the healing of our body. The fact that it is a natural source oil and does not have any psychoactive constituents makes it a perfect choice for many people out there. Though more research is needed to be carried out in this area. The fact that it is not available everywhere makes it a hurdle in the progress of this oil but efforts are already carried out ot legalize it.

If all else fails you can always combine CBD oil's benefits with the knowledge of a registered dietitian and/or certified personal trainer.

Made in United States
Troutdale, OR
08/19/2023

12198245R00040